MONTPELLIER

Simon Barnard
Photographs by Francis de Richemond

Collection The city on foot
(Collection Balades urbaines)

© 2000, Editions Espaces 34
B.P. 2080 - 34025 Montpellier CEDEX 1
Tel.: 04 67 84 11 23
Fax: 04 67 84 00 74

1000 years of history

985 AD: Monte pestelario

The count of Melgueil presented a certain Guilhem with an estate called *Monte pestelario* (the origin of the name Montpellier), but the etymology of the name is still a mystery.

A sanctuary consecrated to Our Lady had been built on the hill where the town was to take form and the Virgin Mary depicted in the Montpellier's first seal still appears in the arms of the city.

Trade developed around the sanctuary and the town began to take shape.

End of the twelfth century

Construction of the ramparts forming the 'Commune Clôture': this corresponded roughly to the boulevards encircling the city centre today. Population: 6,000 to 10,000.

Thirteenth century

Montpellier came under the control of Pedro of Aragon in 1204, after his marriage to 'Marie de Montpellier'. Their son, Jaime I (Spain's 'Jaime El Conquistador'), the hero of 30 victories and the founder of 2,000 churches, was born in Montpellier in 1208.

1349

The 'kings of Majorca period' came to an end when Philippe VI de Valois, king of France, purchased the city for 120,000 gold crowns.

Medieval Montpellier

A centre for crafts (goldsmiths, silversmiths, tanners, weavers and dyers). Spices, sugar, drugs and silk arrived via the port of Lattes on the river Lez and were then transported to fairs all over Europe.

The famous Medical School (founded in 1220), where Rabelais studied medicine, soon accompanied by the law faculty and the theology faculty (1421) did much to make Montpellier famous.

Fifteenth, sixteenth and seventeenth centuries

Montpellier gained the status of provincial capital in the fifteenth and sixteenth centuries, when it became a centre of legal, tax and financial institutions, together with the bishopric, transferred from Maguelone. The wars of religion were felt strongly in Montpellier, which had an important political position in the Languedoc. After various sieges and bouts of demolition, the construction of the fortified Citadelle finally established Louis XIII's control of the city.

Eighteenth century
Installation of the Cour des Aides and the Chambre des Comptes. Splendid mansions were built in the city centre.

Growth of the production of wine and brandy. Manufacture of '*indiennes*' (printed cotton). Tanneries.

The Revolution
A period particularly marked by food shortages. A guillotine was set up on the promenade du Peyrou. The first elected mayor of Montpellier was executed in Paris.

Nineteenth century
The railway line arrived in 1845. Streets were widened and the present rue Foch was driven mercilessly through the tissue of the medieval town centre.

The new state school system succeeded in eliminating the patois that had been spoken by most of the population in 1800.

Founding of the Musée Fabre and construction of the present 'Opéra' (1888).

Twentieth century
Half a century of comparative calm. In 1948, a debate was held on the subject of 'Why Montpellier is dying'.

And then, a sudden awakening: Montpellier was awarded a 'blue ribbon for growth' in 1968 after a 35 percent population increase in just six years, following the massive arrival of French from North Africa after the Algerian War.

Montpellier today
A centre for universities, hospitals, medical research, somewhat hi-tech industries and the Agropolis research centre—devoted principally to Mediterranean and tropical agricultural research—Montpellier is now a flourishing city, attracting all those who wish to live, work and enjoy life in an exceptional setting.

Sculpture (detail) by Injalbert at the entry to the Peyrou

Montpellier

Fontaine des Trois Grâces

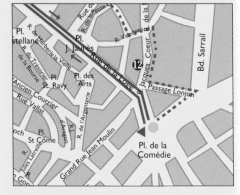

Visit Montpellier on foot in 1 hour, 2 hours or more. Two basic routes are described, with a variety of alternatives. Times are provided as a guide only.

All the walks start at the Trois Graces (the Three Graces), the local emblematic statue, in Place de la Comédie with the Opéra and café terraces, but you can start where you wish and do all or part of a walk in whatever direction you choose. *Bonne promenade*!

WALK 1 – SHORT TOUR

DURATION: ABOUT 1 HOUR, COLOUR: BLUE

Through the heart of the city.

Walk up rue de la Loge, one of the main shopping streets, with place Jean Jaurès on the way, with its colourful café terraces.

Leaving the *préfecture* (large clock at the top) on your right, continue along rue Foch, passing the Palais de Justice (typical nineteenth century façade with imposing columns) and the Arc de Triomphe (page 17). Cross the road to the promenade du Peyrou and go to the other end, either through the middle next to the large bronze statue of Louis XIV on horseback or along the side in the shade of the plane trees. Panoramic views as far as the Cévennes to the north and the sea to the

The promenade du Peyrou (Louis XIV, the château d'eau)

Montpellier

'Cricket cage'

Detail
(château d'eau)

south. Note the magnificent eighteenth century *château d'eau*, triumphantly marking the arrival of the town's water supply in the eighteenth century, and the aqueduct beyond. A curious sundial is set in the ground next to the pool.

Go down the steps to the right of the *château d'eau* and return towards the city centre by way of the lower terrace (fine magnolias) on your left, after going beneath the aqueduct. A plaque marks the spot where the famous photograph of Jean Moulin, hero of the Résistance who had studied law in Montpellier, was taken. A pleasant view of the roofs of the town is interrupted by the new law court complex built in 1995-96 at the expense of the demolition of a *quartier* of small houses.

On leaving the promenade, turn left, walk past the main gate opposite the Arc de Triomphe and, going downhill, cross rue Pitot to boulevard Henri IV, bordered with plane trees. Cross the top of rue du Faubourg St Jaumes at the level of the gate to the Jardin des Plantes (Botanical Gardens, visit approximately 40 minutes, page 10). Cross boulevard Henri IV, walk downhill for about 20 metres and then turn into rue de l'Ecole de Médecine on the right. The School of Medicine is on the left. The hall and the grand staircase are worth a look, as is the view of the nave and towers of the cathedral

Montpellier

Place de la Canourgue

'La coquille'

from the inside courtyard (Musée Atger, page 29). Further along the street, the cathedral porch with its immense pillars. Somewhat less grandiose, a cricket cage, a mini warning system in the centre of the ironwork of one of the balconies of 16 rue St Pierre, deserves attention. Walk up rue St Pierre and the beginning of rue de la Vieille Intendance and then take the wide steps on the right leading to place de la Canourgue, a delight of shade and elegance. In front of you, the 'Unicorn fountain' (1770) by Etienne d'Antoine, with a scene of the Battle of Clostercamp (the death of the valiant Chevalier d'Assas). On your left, hôtel (mansion) Richer de Belleval (second half of the seventeenth century) and, diagonally opposite at the other end of the square at the corner of hôtel de Sarret, *la coquille* (circa 1630), a cleverly hollowed portion of wall, still examined and admired by master stonemasons today.

• To return directly to place de la Comédie: follow rue du Palais next to 'Antidote Café' and then fork right into rue de la Barralerie to return to place des Martyrs de la Résistance (*préfecture*) and walk down rue de la Loge to the starting point.

• Through the old streets (10 minutes longer): from place de la Canourgue, take rue du Palais and then fork left into rue de Ratte. After a few metres, turn right into rue de la Préfecture, which leads immediately into place Chabaneau. The fine Fontaine de l'Intendance (1775) by Journet stands in the centre of the *place*, with a young woman (representing the city of Montpellier) distributing water. Cross the top of rue de l'Université, walk around the Préfecture, keeping it on your left and then leave it when you reach the post office and cross place du Marché aux Fleurs (named after a long-gone flower market) diagonally. Sculpture/fountain by the Catalan sculptor Manuel Clemente Ochoa in the centre of the *place*. Take rue Delpech at the opposite corner between the cafés and then turn right into rue de la Carbonnerie. Turn right again when you reach rue de l'Aiguillerie and then take the second turning to the left (place Pétrarque). Don't miss hôtel de Varennes, restored by the town. It houses the Musée du Vieux Montpellier and the Musée du Fougau (page 29). Walk along rue Embouque d'Or and then down the tiny rue Valedeau and turn right into rue Jacques Coeur (No. 5: hôtel des Trésoriers de France, fifteenth and seventeenth centuries, Musée Languedocien, page 28) and return to place de la Comédie via Passage Lonjon (second turning on the left).

'Creation', a sculpture/ fountain by Clemente Ochoa in place du Marché aux Fleurs

Montpellier

Jardin des Plantes

The opening hours tend to vary. See the notice on the gate.

Montpellier is very lucky to have a 6-hectare botanical garden—founded in 1593 and the oldest in France—right in the centre of the city. Founded as part of the School of Medicine and still managed by the university, its prime function is neither that of public park nor of decorative gardens. However, although it awakes strong passions in any true botanist's breast, it is a very pleasant place for the visitor and an opportunity to admire rare, acclimatised plants.

Brief visit (minimum 40 minutes)
One can easily spend hours in this garden. But here is a quick tour.
Start by the southern gate (at the top of boulevard Henri IV) and walk down the path on the left, bordered by cypresses. On your right, the scientific garden (Candolle's 'systematic' school). The façade of the orangery (1804) is decorated with the signs of the zodiac. Towards the right, you will see a small bridge made of cast iron and wood. Go beneath this to reach 'Narcissa's tomb'. In his poem *Night Thoughts*, the poet Edward Young claims to have buried his step-daughter here secretly in 1736: 'With pious sacrilege a grave I stole'. Whether the story is true or not, this romantic spot was a favourite of the writers Paul Valéry, André Gide, Pierre Louÿs and Valéry Larbaud. Twenty metres further along,

a small vaulted passage on the left leads to the remains of a noria, on which have been placed old marker stones dating back to the founding of the garden.

Go down the steps opposite the ironwork gate protecting the noria to return to the level of the orangery. The magnificent maidenhair or ginkgo tree (*Ginkgo biloba*) to your left was planted in 1795. Turn right and walk to the end of 'Allée de Toscane', flanked by cypresses and large Anduze jars. Go down the steps at the end, walk between two rose beds and up some more steps to 'Allée Cusson' that runs along the top of 'montagne de Richer', restored in the spirit of the founder of the garden and planted with garrigue plants and oaks. In front of you, the famous 'letter-box tree' (it is still used today), an extremely curious *Phillyrea latifolia* as old as the garden. The sprawling Judas tree at the other end of the path is also thought to be just as old.

Turn right towards the 'English garden' with a fine lily pond, the observatory, the 'Martins' greenhouse containing succulents and bougainvilleas, rockeries, bamboos, a collection of

Solanaceae, etc. Walk past the greenhouse and then the rockery. Leaving the Institut de Botanique behind you, take the broad path leading to the monument to François Rabelais and then go up the eastern (left) side of the garden. The Tour des Pins (page 22), topped by cypress trees, is visible on the other side of the wall. The left-hand path takes you back to the gate through which you came into the garden.

Montpellier

Place de la Comédie and the Opéra

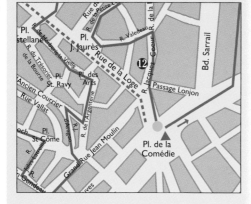

WALK 2 – FULL TOUR

DURATION (without the visit to the Jardin des Plantes): approximately 2h 15 min (SHORTER VERSION: 1h 15 min). COLOUR: RED

A route for enthusiasts who wish to explore the city in more detail.

Start at the Fontaine des Trois Grâces (1773). Turn your back to the theatre (Opéra-Comédie) and walk along Esplanade Charles de Gaulle, with its rows of fine plane trees and a pair of attractive fountains. On the right, the Galerie Photo (page 30) and, behind the monument to Jean Jaurès, Pavillon du Musée Fabre (1890), renovated a few years ago as an exhibition space (temporary exhibitions). The bandstand, one of the first reinforced concrete buildings in Montpellier, stands nearby. Behind, the leafy shade of the peaceful Champ de Mars gardens. Opposite, at 29 boulevard Sarrail, note the superb façade of the former Pathé cinema (1908), now the Centre Rabelais, used for lectures and films during various festivals. Further along the boulevard, hôtel Cabrières-Sabatier d'Espeyran (page 28) forms the corner of rue Montpellieret. Just afterwards, the Musée Fabre (page 27), with a small garden in front, was initially a Jesuits' College (1682). The Corum, a conference centre, opera house, etc. stands at the end of the Esplanade. Steps lead to the roof (add about 10 minutes to the walk) for a broad view westward of the northern side of Montpellier, with the red brick of hôtel de Sully (now the Centre for International Relations) and its small and shady public garden in the foreground.

Walk up rue Girard along the right-hand side of the museum and follow it into rue de la Salle l'Evêque, with a succession of fine mansions (hotel de Girard, hôtel de Grave, etc.). Turn down rue Bocaud on the left; you will reach the top of rue du Pila St-Gély at the level of the Jardin d'Assas. A statue of St Roch is set half-way up a wall opposite (pilgrimage on 16 August). Walk up rue de l'Aiguillerie for about 20 metres then turn right into rue des Ecoles Laïques. This runs though place de la Chapelle Neuve whose restaurant terraces are extremely lively on summer evenings.

You will reach boulevard Louis-Blanc, freshly paved for Montpellier's new tram line. Turn left and walk along the former Ursuline convent, now a choreographic centre. The building dates back to 1647, but with major modifications

Hôtel de Grave

*Place de la
Chapelle Neuve*

Montpellier

Les Ursulines

School of Medicine, entry

(the present façade and the semi-circular portion) in 1805.

After Les Ursulines, turn left through the old city gate (porte de la Blanquerie, 1785) and walk up rue de l'Université. Notice the Law Faculty at No. 39 (formerly a convent) and the former Hôtel-Dieu Saint-Éloi (hospital) at No. 31 (now used for education administration offices).

Turn into rue de Candolle on the right. This is a very old quarter with a strong gypsy tradition. Take a moment to admire the fine sculpture, *Paradis perdu* (Paradise Lost) by Jacques Augustin Dieudonné in the centre of Plan de l'Université and don't miss the fine seventeenth century door of No. 20, opposite the statue.

Keep straight on and you reach rue St-Pierre and the vast bulk of the cathedral in front of you. You can't miss it. However, you have to look closely to find the cricket cage, a mini warning system set in the centre of the ironwork of one of the balconies of 16 rue St-Pierre. Cross the cobbled area in front of the cathedral and climb the stairs to rue de l'Ecole de Médecine. The School of Medicine, where François Rabelais enrolled in 1530, adjoins the cathedral. The door is flanked by two imposing nineteenth century statues. It is worth going through the hall to the inner court-

*Paradise Lost
(Candolle
quarter)*

Montpellier

*St Clement
aqueduct
('les Arceaux')*

yard for a good view of the cathedral towers and nave. Continue and then turn left up boulevard Henri IV and cross it at the traffic lights. This brings you to one of the gates to the Jardin des Plantes (visit described on page 10). Keep walking uphill, crossing rue du Faubourg St-Jaumes and then rue Pitot to reach the main gate to the Promenade du Peyrou (Page 19). Cross to the other end, either through the middle next to the large bronze statue of Louis XIV on horseback or along the side in the shade of the plane trees. Note the *château d'eau* (completed in 1774), Saint-Clément aqueduct, commonly referred to as 'les Arceaux' (completed in 1762) and—especially for children—the curious twentieth century sundial set in the ground in front of the pool at the end of the promenade.

Go down the steps to the right of the *château d'eau* and return towards the city centre by way of the lower terrace (fine magnolias) on your left, after going beneath the aqueduct. A plaque marks the spot where the famous photograph of Jean Moulin, hero of the Résistance who had studied law in Montpellier, was taken. Pleasant view of the roofs of the town interrupted by the new law court complex built in 1995-96 at the expense of the demolition of a *quartier* of small houses.

The Arc de Triomphe

Built as the 'Porte du Peyrou' (Peyrou gate) in 1691 on the site of an old gate and drawbridge, the latter being replaced by a stone bridge, the arch was subsequently consecrated to the glory of Louis XIV. Carved medallions depict episodes of his long reign. On the Peyrou side, on the left, the king is represented as Hercules dominating a dragon (England) and frightening away the Austrian eagle; the victories of Mons and Namur are illustrated on the right. On the city side, you can see the building of the Canal du Midi and finally the revocation of the Edict of Nantes. The Latin inscription was carved in 1715, the year of the death of Louis XIV, and can be translated as follows: 'Louis the Great ruled for 72 years and, in a war lasting four decades, separated, repressed and reunited peoples, bringing peace on land and at sea. 1715'.

Montpellier

St Anne's church

On leaving the promenade, turn left and then cross the road, keeping to the right of the Arc de Triomphe (opposite). You are in rue Foch, the result of a Haussmann style 'demolish and rebuild' operation towards the end of the nineteenth century. The street was to have gone right through to the Esplanade (but the cash ran out). The Palais de Justice is on the left, opposite rue de la Valfère. A thousand years ago, the *Val Fère* was a thick wood full of wild beasts. There are mainly lawyers there today.

• Short route: Return directly to place de la Comédie along rue Foch and then rue de la Loge

• To continue the full tour: Walk along rue Foch for about 200 metres and then turn into rue du Petit Scel on the right, leading to place du Petit Scel and its mossy fountain. St Anne's church—nineteenth century gothic—is now Carré Sainte-Anne, an exhibition space. The Conservatoire is opposite the church with an adjoining '...structure of indeterminate provenance decorated with antique style motifs...'. A medieval house (note the windows) can be seen downhill from the *place*, towards the right. Keep the church on your left and walk down rue Sainte-Anne (along the row of trees) and then cross rue St-Guilhem and take narrow rue de

Promenade du Peyrou

Brief history

Laid out in 1689 by d'Aviler, who had studied under Jules Hardouin-Mansart, the 'Peyrou' was initially a large rectangle 175 m long and 125 m wide, used as a promenade and for festivals. A large statue of Louis XIV erected in 1718 was demolished and melted down during the Revolution, when a guillotine was the main attraction. The statue was replaced by a smaller version in 1828.

Enormous civil engineering works were carried out in the eighteenth century to bring water to the town by means of the St Clément Aqueduct that finishes by 'Les Arceaux' and the Peyrou, with the fine *château d'eau* (by Giral). The lower terraces and the fountains on either side of the last three arches of the aqueduct were added at that time.

The Peyrou today

With a broad view to the north—the Pic St Loup and the Cévennes beyond—and to the west—the Gardiole hill on the coast—the Peyrou is a popular place for mothers and children, afternoon strollers, readers and, more recently, African drum enthusiasts! It is the perfect place for taking a rest when you are visiting Montpellier. There are plenty of benches around the edge of the promenade. Have fun with the sundial set in the ground next to the pool (a favourite for water-loving dogs).

One can cross the Peyrou and go down the steps towards place des Arceaux and the *quartier* of the same name. On Saturday mornings, a 'collectors' market (books, coins etc.) and a mainly organic fruit and vegetable market are set up along the aqueduct.

Montpellier

Rue de l'Ancien Courrier

Hôtel St-Côme (right)

l'Ancien Courrier opposite, a pedestrian street since the 1960s. Don't miss one of the entries to hôtel de Montcalm at No. 3. After about 50 metres, turn right and go down rue des Soeurs Noires. Leaving St Roch's church on the left, follow rue des Soeurs Noires which angles to the right, leading to rue du Puits du Temple; the 'Knight Templars' well' is in front of you, behind a window, at the corner of rue des Teissiers. Walk up the latter street to the steps in front of St Roch's church. Continue opposite along rue St-Côme to place St-Côme, with the magnificent dome of the Saint-Côme anatomy theatre (1691-1711). Do not cross the *place*, but turn right down rue Jules Latreille, left into rue En-Gondeau and then right when you reach Grand'Rue Jean Moulin, one of the main shopping streets. Walk down to the boulevard. This was the site of one of the main city gates (Porte de la Saunerie) in the Middle Ages. Turn left along boulevard de l'Observatoire as far as Tour de la Babote, a vestige of the fortifications, and go through the gate into the courtyard. Cross and leave by the iron gate in rue Diderot. Turn left and walk along to rue des Etuves, where, opposite but slightly to the left, a cannonball reputed to have been fired during the 1622 siege

Tour de la Babote

A large corner tower in the medieval fortifications. It was made higher in the fourteenth century and changed considerably in the eighteenth century, with the construction of an observatory by the Société Royale des Sciences. The gate was made in the tower when the outer ditch was filled in at the end of the eighteenth century.

The various functions of the tower included that of Chappe telegraph (semaphore) station until 1855. It is also claimed that a certain Lenormand leaped off the top for the first parachute jump in history.

Montpellier

WALKS

Tour des Pins

Set in a cool garden, Tour des Pins is next to boulevard Henri IV (east of the Jardin des Plantes, near the cathedral) It is a remnant (lower part only) of the 'Commune Clôture' completed in 1196. This tower and Tour de la Babote are all that remain of 25 towers and 8 gates along the fortifications. Pines grew on the top of it for centuries but, when they began to cause serious damage to the masonry, were replaced by cypresses to guard against Nostradamus prediction: 'The town will perish when the pines on the tower have gone'.

is lodged in the wall above the door to No. 30. Keep straight on until you reach Grand'Rue and walk up it (to the right) as far as hotel St-Côme, now the Chamber of Commerce, whose dome you have already seen from the *place* behind it. Angle to the left (rue En-Rouan) and go along narrow rue Jacques d'Aragon on the right as far as Plan Pastourel. Jaime of Aragon was born here in 1208 in Tournemire Palace (where No. 2 rue Jacques d'Aragon now stands). Turn right and walk along the last few metres of rue de l'Ancien Courrier. Turn left into rue de l'Argenterie, the old silversmiths' quarter, and walk up towards rue de la Loge. You will pass the recently restored hôtel hostelier Saint-Jean, a former meeting place for Protestants, on the right and then the so-called Palais des Rois d'Aragon on the left in Place des Arts. Just after this, turn left into rue de la Vieille and then take rue St-Ravy to the left, leading to the pleasant place St-Ravy (Galerie Municipale Saint Ravy—exhibitions). Cross the *place* and take rue des Trésoriers de la Bourse to the right. Don't miss hôtel des Trésoriers de la Bourse at No. 4 (open during the week), from where the finances of the Languedoc were managed from 1710 until the French Revolution. Peep into the second courtyard, where the sky

*Place St-Ravy
(left)*

Rue de la Vieille

Montpellier

Hôtel des Trésoriers de la Bourse (first courtyard)

suddenly seems wider after the narrow streets. Rue des Trésoriers de la Bourse finishes at place Castellane behind the covered market. The picturesque rue du Bras de Fer leads off to the left (worth a small detour). Cross the *place* diagonally leaving the market on your right and then cross the top of rue de la Loge. The *préfecture* is opposite you. Walk between the *préfecture* and the post office to reach place du Marché aux Fleurs (but the flower market was moved years ago). Sculpture/fountain by the Catalan sculptor Manuel Clemente Ochoa in the centre of the *place*. Go around the *préfecture* along rue Bonnier d'Alco and rue Cambacérès to reach place Chabaneau. The fine Fontaine de l'Intendance (1775) by Journet stands in the centre of the *place*, with a young woman (representing the city of Montpellier) distributing water. Take the tiny rue de la Préfecture at the rear of the place, turn left along rue de Ratte and then follow rue du Palais des Guilhem to place de la Canourgue, bordered with southern nettle-trees and plane trees. To your left, at the corner of rue de la Coquille, you can see *la coquille* ('the shell') itself (circa 1630), a masterly hollowed masonry construction that has fascinated visitors for 300 years. At the other extremity of the

place, the 'Unicorn fountain' (1770) by Etienne d'Antoine, with a scene of the Battle of Clostercamp (the death of the valiant Chevalier d'Assas), moved from rue de la Loge in 1865. On the right, notice the fine façade of hôtel Richer de Belleval (second half of the seventeenth century), used as the town hall from 1817 to 1971. Go down the broad steps on the right at the end of the *place* and walk along rue Vieille Intendance to rue de l'Université, going past

*Rue Bras de Fer (left)
Fontaine de l'Intendance (detail)*

Montpellier

WALKS

hôtel d'Audessan, or hôtel de la Vieille Intendance (first half of the seventeenth century). Cross rue de l'Université, go down a little way and take rue Fournarié and then rue de Girone and rue de la Carbonnerie as far as rue de l'Aiguillerie. Turn right and then turn into place Pétrarque, the second on the left, where hôtel de Varennes houses the Musée du Vieux Montpellier and the Musée du Fougau (page 29). Take the very narrow rue de la Petite Loge leading off to the right at the end of the *place*. This takes you to place Jean Jaurès and its cafés. Keep left and walk down rue Collot in the left-hand corner and then go down the extremely short rue Valedeau and turn right along rue Jacques Coeur (No. 5: hôtel des Trésoriers de France, fifteenth and seventeenth centuries, now the Musée Languedocien, page 28). Continue to rue de la Loge and turn left to return to your point of departure. Well done!

Place Jean Jaurès (the crypt of Notre-Dame des Tables is beneath the 'place')

MUSEUMS

Musée Fabre

39 boulevard Bonne Nouvelle (Esplanade)
Tel. 04 67 14 83 00
Tuesday to Friday: 9 a.m. to 5.30 p.m.; Saturday and Sunday: 9.30 a.m. to 5 p.m. Closed on Monday.

A very useful map of the museum is provided at the entry. A lift goes to all floors except the Galerie des Colonnes. All the rooms are accessible to disabled persons.

Temporary exhibitions are held in the Pavillon du Musée Fabre on the Esplanade.

Founded in 1828 with the contents of the 120 crates of the personal collection of the painter François-Xavier Fabre — part of this consisted of the collection of Louise de Stolberg, Countess of Albany, widow of Charles James Stuart, a close friend of Fabre in Florence — the musée Fabre contains fabulous treasures.

The Musée Fabre

A few highlights

Everybody is there — Veronese, Bruegel, Bernini, Cousin, Poussin, Zurbarán, Rubens, Le Sueur, Bourdon, Dutch and Flemish works of the Valedeau collection, Greuze, Vernet, Vien (born in Montpellier), Joshua Reynolds, Fabre himself of course, Géricault, Delacroix (8 paintings, gifts of the patron of the arts Alfred Bruyas, referred to as a '...red-bearded narcissist...' with '...a curious passion for being painted' in a modern guide), Corot, Bonington, Courbet, Fromentin and Bazille (a Montpellier painter who died tragically at the age of 29). The twentieth century is represented by Valadon, Utrillo,

Montpellier

Matisse, Bissière, de Staël, Vieira da Silva, Marquet, Dufy and sculptures by Maillol and Germaine Richier. Without forgetting the excellent southern painters such as Desnoyer, the painter of Sète, 'who knows how to see simply and who knows how to see big' (Jean Cassou), Descossy, the Catalan of Montpellier, and Soulages (recent acquisitions).

Level 2: European ceramics and archaeology. Magnificent faience from Montpellier and elsewhere, Greek vases and a splendid carved sarcophagus from Argelliers, decorated with bunches of grapes and doves. Don't miss the enormous oven built into the wall.

From the collection of the Musée Languedocien

Hôtel de Cabrières-Sabatier d'Espeyran
6 bis, rue Montpellieret
Visits by appointment (musée Fabre).
Built in 1872, it houses a collection of furniture and objets d'art, all left to the city in 1957.

Musée Languedocien
(Société Archéologique de Montpellier)
Hôtel des Trésoriers de France,
7 rue Jacques Cœur
Tel. 04 67 52 93 03
Open Monday to Saturday from 2 to 5 p.m. and from 3 to 6 p.m. from the end of June to 31 August (closed on Sundays and public holidays).

Very varied collections of interesting items in a pleasant fifteenth century mansion. Church sculptures from St-Guilhem-le-Désert, Fontfroide Abbey, Saint-Pons and Psalmody and a display of Visigoth objects. You can't miss the huge twelfth century font in the courtyard. The first floor houses a Gothic room, collections of faience, including yellow and blue and white pots made in Montpellier and nineteenth century rooms. The bright rooms on the second floor contain a profusion of prehistoric, protohistoric (Bronze and Iron ages) and Gallo-Roman objects, a magnificent Celtic funerary stele, Greek vases and Estruscan and Egyptian pieces.

Musée du Fougau

(a private museum belonging to the Escolo dau Parage association whose prime purpose is the promotion of *langue d'Oc*)

Hôtel de Varennes, place Pétrarque

Wednesday and Thursday, 3 – 6 p.m. Usually closed from 14 July to 15 August but contact the Office de Tourisme to arrange visits for groups (even small ones). Free entry.

A nice little museum. A collection of all sorts of different things, like splendid earthenware from St-Jean-de-Fos, a club for killing rabbits, a superb nineteenth century silk dress, a velocipede and regular's soap dish at the barber's. An interesting glimpse of what everyday life used to be like in the Languedoc.

Musée du Vieux Montpellier

Hôtel de Varennes, place Pétrarque

Tuesday to Saturday, 9.30 a.m. – 12, 1.30 – 5 p.m. Free entry.

A museum devoted to the history of Montpellier. Various pieces of furniture, including a cupboard for archives from the Tour des Pins (Municipal Records). Engravings and lithographs of historical scenes and various portraits of Montpellier worthies.

Musée d'Anatomie

Faculté de Médecine, rue de l'École de Médecine

Wednesday afternoon, 2.30 – 5 p.m. Free entry.

Not for the squeamish.

Cross the entry hall of the School of Medicine to the terrace. Go through the door to your left and follow the signs.

Old anatomical collections (the museum was founded in 1851): preserved cross sections, dried items, normal and abnormal skulls, skeletons of all sizes, wax items, surgical instruments and a collection of shells, all in a series of rooms with painted ceilings.

Musée Atger

Faculté de Médecine, rue de l'École de Médecine

Monday, Wednesday and Friday, 1.30 – 5.30 p.m.

Closed in August. Free entry.

Cross the entry hall of the School of Medicine to the terrace. Go through the door to your left and follow the signs.

A magnificent collection left by the collector Jean François Xavier Atger (1758-1833).

Some 500 drawings are stored in cabinets. A magnificent Donatello can be found in 'Italiens XVIe-XVIIIe'. A dozen drawings by Tiepolo, including a superb head of an old man and two sheets of studies of heads. Annibale Carracci, Watteau, Fragonard, Poussin, Bourdon and Vien. Not to be missed by art-lovers.

Video on Atger in French and in English.

La Galerie Photo

Esplanade Charles de Gaulle

Often excellent temporary exhibitions.

Montpellier

The Corum (top)
The new Antigone
quarter

MUSEUMS OUTSIDE THE CITY CENTRE

Musée des Moulages
Université Paul Valéry, route de Mende
Wednesday to Saturday, 1.30 – 5.30 p.m.. Closed in August.
Free entry.
One of the best collections of plaster casts in France.
Three thousand years of classical antiquity.

Musée montpelliérain de la Pharmacie
Faculté de Pharmacie, avenue Charles Flahaut
Tel. 04 67 54 80 00
Tuesday and Friday, 10 a.m. - 12
Free entry.
Small museum stuffed with fascinating objects.

Agropolis Museum
951 avenue Agropolis
Tel. 04 67 04 75 14
Tram to St.-Éloi and then the Agropolis Lavalette *navette*
(bus shuttle service). Every day except Tuesday, 2 – 6 p.m.
Permanent exhibition on farming and food around the world.

Musée de l'Infanterie
École d'Application de l'Infanterie, avenue Lepic
Tel. 04 67 07 21 10
Every day except Tuesday, 2 – 6 p.m.
French infantry from 1479 to the present day.

WHERE TO GO WITHOUT A CAR

Zoo
Parc Zoologique Henri de Lunaret.
A magnificent 'open' zoo in 80 hectares of garrigue, criss-crossed by footpaths. You tend to come across animals as you go round a corner and you can even take a picnic. Entry is free, thanks to Henri de Lunaret who bequeathed this magnificent piece of land to the town. Open every day (winter: 8 a.m. – 5 p.m.; summer: 8 a.m. – 7 p.m.).

Take the tram to Saint-Eloi, and then the Agropolis Lavalette bus shuttle (*navette*). Bus stop at the zoo.

Bois de Montmaur
Run and do exercises in the garrigue. Opposite the zoo (access as above – same bus stop).

Swimming pool
(piscine olympique d'Antigone)
195 avenue Jacques Cartier, Antigone
Tel. 04 67 15 63 00
Monday to Friday 9 a.m. – 8 p.m. and 8.30 p.m. – 10 p.m.; Saturday 9 a.m. – 7 p.m.; Sundays and holidays 9 a.m. – 1 p.m. and from 3 p.m. – 7 p.m.
On foot from the city centre or take the tram (towards Odysseum, the southern terminus).

Flea market at La Paillade
Enormous flea market every Sunday until 1 p.m. in the La Mosson football stadium car park.

Take the tram to the northern terminus (Mosson) or bus 15 from the city centre.

The flea market at La Paillade

Flower market
Plants of all kinds, trees, etc. Every Tuesday until 5 p.m. in the La Mosson football stadium car park.
Take the tram to the northern terminus (Mosson) or bus 15 from the city centre.

Ice skating rink
A new complex with two skating rinks, cafeteria etc. Late opening is planned.
Take the tram to the southern terminus (Odysseum).

The sea
By bus from the bus station:
Courriers du Midi, Tel. 04 67 06 03 67
TaM, Tel. 04 67 22 87 87

INFORMATION

Office de tourisme
Place de la Comédie (towards Triangle/Polygone)
Tel. 04 67 60 60 60 Fax: 04 67 60 60 61
web site: www.ot-montpellier.fr
e-mail: contact@ot-montpellier.fr
Tourist and hotel information. Guided tours.

Transport
Railway station: Place Auguste Gilbert,
    Tel. 04 99 74 15 10
Bus station: rue Jules Ferry,
    Tel. 04 67 92 01 43
Montpellier-Méditerranée airport:
    Tel. 04 67 20 85 85
Airport coach shuttle: Courriers du Midi,
    Tel. 04 67 06 03 67

Emergency numbers
SAMU (emergency medical service): 15
Police: 17
Fire Brigade: 18
European emergency number: 112
SOS Médecin (doctors 24 hours a day):
    Tel. 04 67 72 22 15
Médecins 24 h/24 h (doctors 24 hours a day):
    Tel. 04 67 59 92 92

Simon Barnard has lived in Montpellier for over 25 years. He is a translator and has written tourist guides and children's books.

Francis de Richemond was born in Montpellier and has taken photographs for numerous books about the city. He has published several hiking guides, with detailed circuits within 100 km of Montpellier and has one of the largest photo libraries in Languedoc-Roussillon.

Graphic design: Karen Lehrer, 34270 Claret

Printed by: Maury - 12100 Millau